Conversational Hypnosis

in Action — Influence on the go.

A Manual of Practical Influence Skills to

Inspire Others & Enrich Your Life

Disclaimer and Legal Notices

All the information in this book is for entertainment purposes only and Keys To The Mind, takes no responsibility for any errors, inaccuracies or omissions. You are fully encouraged to do further research before acting on the basis of the information in this book.

This book stresses that you should use the ideas herein for the benefit of others only, and incorporate the persuasive strategies described ethically and judiciously for the mutual benefit of all involved.

This is not a book on therapy or therapeutic technique, and anyone wishing to practice therapy formally or otherwise should seek professional training.

This entire book is copyrighted (c) Keys To The Mind – no parts may be reproduced, shared or distributed in any form without explicit written consent from the owner.

Welcome to Conversational Hypnosis in Action – Influence on the go

I am writing this book to give you practical persuasion tools that will allow you to enrich your life, as well as the lives of those around you.

This book is (emphatically) not long. I do not believe in waffling on for pages andpages about abstract theory, aiming to bulk up the book so I can bulk up the price tag.

No, this book is about what you get out of it.

By the time you finish reading this, you will understand how to communicate with people on a level that really makes an impact.

You'll be able to brush aside the objections and interruptions that you've been facing up until now, and actually get through to people in a way that makes a difference.

I'm sure you'll love this book, as much thought, much work and over 6 years research has gone into it, and we welcome your feedback and reactions.

Laying the Foundation, Then Building the Skyscraper

The first few chapters of this book will focus on the "inner game."

This is the foundation of effective persuasion, and is by far the most important part of this book.

Let me say that again:

The inner game is by far the most important part of this book!

Skip it and move straight to techniques, and you'll only be sabotaging yourself.

The inner game is the foundation. Take the time to build a solid foundation, and on top of it you'll be able to construct a magnificent skyscraper.

Without a solid inner game, techniques have no power.

If you've struggled in the past with hypnosis or persuasion despite having perfect technique, you had better believe that it was lack of *inner game foundations* that made the difference!

Covert Hypnosis Made Simple

People often ask me if there's a difference between conversational hypnosis and covert hypnosis.

Well, yes and no. Technically conversational hypnosis is any form of hypnotic influence that occurs during a conversation; that can be, but does not necessarily have to be, covert.

Covert hypnosis, on the other hand, is any influence that occurs without the conscious awareness of the person being influenced. That does not necessarily have to occur during a conversation.

If that doesn't make sense, don't worry about it. For all intents and practicalities, the two are one and the same thing.

Now before we move on, let's quickly clear up this idea of *hypnosis.* Hypnosis is frighteningly misunderstood, not just by the public, but also (most worryingly) by hypnotists.

Let's put all the superstition and exaggeration out of our minds for the time being, and look at hypnosis as *any influence that occurs at the subconscious level.*
Understand this as any change that occurs at the level of emotions, imagination and habits.

Basically: Any real and powerful change that you create.

So, in this book you're going to learn how to

create real, powerful changes within ordinary conversations.

Standing On The Shoulders of Giants: Milton Erickson, NLP and Beyond

Many people say "Conversational Hypnosis is just NLP in a new package."

NLP or "Neuro Linguistic Programming" is a system of modelling which aims to break down the behaviours of successful people into techniques we can all copy.

NLP is best known for its modelling of therapists such as the famous hypnotist Milton Erickson.

Milton Erickson was known for *indirect hypnosis*, creating incredible transformations in his clients through merely telling stories laden with covert hypnotic devices.

NLP created many techniques from this modelling, such as embedded commands, hypnotic language patterns and beyond.

However, NLP is *not* the last word on conversational hypnosis – particularly not the way I teach it!

I agree with Milton Erickson, when he said:

"NLP got me down to a nutshell. Unfortunately, they left out the nut, and only took the shell."

In this book, we'll be going beyond Erickson and looking at many more people who were masters of influence, from monarchs to billionaires and best selling writers.

Rather than teaching the shell of one man's brilliance, we will be, as the physicist says, standing on the shoulders of many giants.

The Win:Win Formula. How to Get Your Own Way and Still Be a Good Person

Some people come to conversational hypnosis from a very unhealthy place.

They want to gain tools and techniques to "trick" others, to get one over on them and manipulate them for their own benefit.

Some trainers also have the same perspective. It's sad to see so many people squirm when they try and strip the negative connotations away from the word 'manipulation,' it's like trying to strip the connotations of 'wet' away from the word 'water!'

In order to be an effective persuader of people – to be looked up to, trusted and responded to, you need to come at this from a perspective of **Win:Win**.

If you benefit to someone else's detriment by

tricking them, even if they don't realize it, you haven't won.

Why? Because people are smarter than you give them credit for! At some level they'll realize that they've been taken for a ride, and next time around they'll be far less likely to trust you.

People are amazingly perceptive when it comes to intuitive judgments of others.

When I was a kid living at my Mother's house, we had a new neighbour, who I took an instant dislike to.

I couldn't explain why, but whenever she came near me I just got creeped out. No one else openly shared my gut feelings, however I stayed adamant.

A couple of months later the rest of my family started gradually cottoning on. The neighbour would start imposing on us for this and that, borrowing things and not returning them, and generally being a nuisance.

Eventually, due to unwise words and unwelcome deeds, she alienated the entire street.

Why did I get that gut instinct?

Something in her body language and demeanour must have told me that this person just was not to be trusted.

I'm sure you've had the same reaction: ever just meet someone and, without any apparent explanation, feel an instant sense of dislike toward them?

The same process works in reverse, of course. Sometimes you meet people and instantly you just want to know them better and be around them more.

Using "covert hypnosis" to others' detriment will show at some level in the way you behave and act.

Using covert hypnosis to help others will have the opposite effect, and people will love you for it.

As you'll come to realize as you read more of this book, it is actually easier to get your own way when you help others get theirs!

So, go forth without guilt or worry! The more you learn about how to get what you want from life, the more the people you care about and deal with will benefit too.

The stories in the next chapter will bring this message home particularly powerfully, and teach you a lesson in persuasion that seems simple, yet is unbelievably powerful.

(Use This Space For Notes and Ideas – I know you've been having them!)

Persuasion Secrets from A Millionaire, A Billionaire, and the Queen of England

My father used to tell me a great story about Queen Victoria.

I'm not sure if it's true, and even if it is, I've long since forgotten the details, but I remember the essence.

The Lesson from the Queen

The Queen was hoping to appoint someone to a position of power, and had two fine candidates to choose from.

The first candidate came to their meeting with flair and charisma.

He was passionate and persuasive, and left the young Queen incredibly impressed.

When her husband Albert asked her how the meeting went, she said, "It was amazing! He made me believe that he is the most important person in the world!"

The next day the Queen met with the second candidate. He was a little quieter, a little less "impressive."

He talked well, but as well as telling grand stories he also asked questions, and listened intently.

Very soon, the Queen found herself talking to him as if he were an old friend.

That night Prince Albert again asked how the meeting went. The Queen smiled and said "It was amazing! He made me believe that *I* am the most important person in the world."

Now, who do you think the Queen choose to appoint?

The Millionaire and Bestselling Author

Stephen R Covey, who recently passed away, wrote a phenomenal book called "*7 Habits of Highly Effective People.*"

It still lines the book shelves of nearly every executive in the Western World and beyond, and sold close to 20 million copies during his lifetime.

Covey founded a consulting company that had a stack of Fortune 500 companies and eminent businesses as clients, and still thrives now.

There were many secrets to his success, but one of the most striking is also one of the 7 habits.

It is this:

Seek first to understand, then to be understood.

In that order. It is truly staggering how many people get this the wrong way around or, more often than not, completely ignore step one!

Seek first to understand, then to be understood.

Tattoo that on your forehead, because it will change your life!

The Billionaire and Wall Street Tycoon

Bernard Baruch was born in 1870. He made a fortune as an investor, and spent his old age as a highly regarded political consultant, advising President Woodrow Wilson, among others.

Bernard Baruch knew how to get his own way, and even Presidents and Prime Ministers rushed to do what he advised.

He had one rule, one secret, and it's very simple. Here's roughly how he put it:

You find out what people want, then you show them how to get it.

This is another saying you'll want to tattoo on your soon to be very sore forehead:

You find out what people want, then you show them how to get it.

What These Three Have in Common

The Queen, the Millionaire and the Billionaire all impart pretty much the same lesson. *Make people feel important.*

Understand who they are. Find out what they

want, and teach them how to get it. It seems very,

very simple.

Alarmingly, most people do NONE of the above.

It's easy to consciously think "Oh yeah,

seek first to understand – gotcha." In

reality, of course, the ego gets in the way.

People clamour to make their voice heard, get their point across and try and seem like *they* are the centre of the universe.

Whilst you are in all probability the centre of *your* universe, don't make the mistake of believing you're the centre of everyone else's as well!

This really does take practice. So, make a conscious effort.

Tattooing on the forehead is a bit extreme I admit, but how's this: Write out these three phrases on separate bits of paper:

- *Make Them Feel Important*
- *You find out what people want, then you show them how to get it.*
- *Seek first to understand, then to be understood.*

And stick each bit of paper somewhere obvious so that you'll see them every day; your bedroom wall, beside your desk, on the fridge.

Make these three rules *habits*, not just catchy phrases, and it will totally change your life.

Go ahead and do that now, and I'll see you on the next chapter.

Getting Out of Your Own Way

When you ask someone what are their barriers to persuading others, you'll hear a bunch of 'excuses.'

Are any of these familiar?

- People are stubborn

- They just won't listen

- They never let me get a word in!

- They judge me before they know me

- I never had a chance

- They just didn't want to hear it

Push past the outer layer, get them to relent a little and then you'll hear deeper spin off 'self excuses.' Things like:

- I'm just not confident

- I'm shy

- I'm not a persuasive person

- People just don't like me

- I am not one of 'those guys.' Ring any

bells?

These excuses aren't real. They're not set in stone. They're not *facts.* They're just beliefs. And beliefs can be changed, as you'll very soon learn! In order to become a successful persuader, it's time to get out of your own way and kick these beliefs to the curb.

Reference Experiences

When you develop a belief, it starts with a suspicion, and then it gets fed.
One failure after another may have compounded the belief in you, or someone you know, that *"I'm just not a persuasive person."*

This belief then sabotages their behaviour, and they act in a way that *confirms* that belief. It becomes a self fulfilling prophecy. So the first step is **change your filter.**

Change the way you process, interpret, and frame

events in your life.

Rather than interpreting a failure as an all conclusive statement about who you are, just think "I learned something useful."

Laugh it off, take the lessons, and move on.

As soon as you've *reframed failure* into something positive – a learning experience, then things suddenly get flipped upside down.

It's a quick and easy shift to make, but it's something you have to put energy into to let it sink in.

Sure, you've heard it before, but has it really clicked?

Failure doesn't *mean* anything except for the fact that you're learning. Got it? Ok, then what happens?

With this change of filter, rather than collecting "proof" of your old limiting beliefs, you collect learning experiences and ideas to improve your persuasive powers.

You then start getting BETTER at this, which means gradually you start achieving some successes.

The more successes you achieve, the more *reference experiences* you have that begin to confirm this positive belief that says "*I am a master persuader.*"

Eventually, this belief becomes a reality, and the

whole process builds itself into a naturally evolving cycle.

It all begins with that one quick simple and easy change in filter and like a snowball rolling down a mountain, the new positive belief goes to work for itself!

Now don't think too hard on this.
Relax and let it sink in now and remind yourself of it every now and then, but for the most part just keep on doing your thing, without forcing yourself to analyse every little event.

Now, I can guess what many of you are thinking at this point...

"Well, that's all very well for the OTHER people who read this book, but you know I'm special. I've got this secret problem that none of you could even IMAGINE."

Hmmmm. Sound about right?

Many people have this 'secret limitation' or 'excuse' hidden away in their mind, preventing them from getting out of their own way and moving forward.

But remember this ancient personal development adage:

The More Personal The Problem, The More Universal

So the more you think your hidden deep and secret excuse is unique to you, the more everyone else probably has a similar "unique" excuse of their own!

So get over it (whatever it is!) and get out of your own way!
Ok, I think I've used up my exclamation mark

quota for this book, so let's move right along and

look at the ever so crucial art of *rapport.*

Effortless Rapport That Forms a Deep Connection

If you want to persuade someone, you

have to get them on your side. Well,

you don't *have to* but it's certainly

easier that way.

Rapport is a connection between two people, when your attention is on each other and you feel as if you're 'on the same wavelength.'

Productive meetings where change takes place are caused by rapport.

You've experienced this *state* of rapport many times in the past, when you've been talking to friends and enjoying their company, or having a really good, deep conversation.

Rapport isn't just one on one of course; a good speaker connects with his audience. In other words, a good speaker engages in *rapport* with his or her audience.

So, how do we create this "rapport?"

At the start of this book I talked to you about NLP. NLP, the process of modelling successful behaviours to derive techniques and patterns, is **big** on rapport.

The trouble is I think they got it wrong.

They teach that if you want to get in rapport with someone, you *match and mirror.*

You subtly mimic their body language, movements and gestures to subconsciously project that you two are alike.

NLP has a host of tricks to make this process more subtle, but at the most basic level that's what it boils down to.

How did NLP come to the conclusion that reflecting gestures is the key to successful communication?

Simple: they watched. Go to a cafe or coffee shop or bar, and watch all the cliques in action.

Look at the intimate couples and the laughing friends and observe the body language.

You'll find that they often are adopting the same pose, sitting the same way. That's a great observation, *but* the process doesn't necessarily work in reverse.

Sure, being in rapport may cause you to mirror each other's body language, but mirroring each other's body language does not necessarily cause you to be in rapport.

It's like saying that rich people spend a lot of money; therefore, in order to be rich, you have to spend a lot of money!

Now, to give NLP its due, there is a *little* sense behind matching and mirroring body language.

After all, physiology
does affect state of
mind.
Leanback in your chair
now, *smile* and look
relaxed.

Hold that relaxed, smiling pose for 30 seconds, making it look as realistic as possible.

Chances are you'll begin to feel good as a result? You're triggering physiological associations to happiness.

However, true happiness comes from a **lot** more things than just changing your body language.

True rapport also is caused by a **lot** more factors than just changing your body language!

• Note for the angry NLPers: Sensible people would not believe the barrage of angry emails I get whenever I dispel an NLP myth. No doubt this book will elicit a few.

Good. You bought this to learn new things, right? So I'd be doing you a disservice if I just stuck to the old fashioned beliefs and taught stuff the same as everyone else.

Read this with an open mind, and if it challenges your beliefs, that's ok! Learning comes from embracing new perspectives, but it would be hubris if I said that every word in this book was gospel. For now, try it on and see how you can make these ideas and techniques useful.

How to Really Create Good Rapport

So now that I've put you right on the old matching and mirroring myth, let's look at how to actually create good rapport.

You know what, it's actually time to go back to basics.
Dale Carnegie (author of "How to Win Friends and Influence People") basics.

Rapport is a *connection,* so stop thinking about fancy techniques, and get out there and start *connecting!*

The biggest thing that stops students of conversational hypnosis from succeeding with rapport is this:

They Try Too Hard!

You can't *force* friendship, and you can't *force* rapport.
Trying only cancels out the subtle, natural

processes that are occurring behind the scenes. Trying means you start consciously sabotaging a subconscious process.

It's like *trying* to force yourself to fall asleep and *willing* yourself unconscious – it just does not work!

BUT you can *create* rapport – and you can deliberately make it happen in *almost* all cases.

So, here's my four step rapport formula:

The Four Step Rapport Formula
1. Visit a Tattoo Parlour!

Ok, not *literally*.
But, do revisit the earlier chapter where I taught you the secrets from the millionaire, the billionaire and the Queen of England.
Remember the three phrases that I told you to Tattoo on your forehead?

They are 110% the key to rapport – putting them to work alone will put you head and shoulders above 99% of the planet!

This Becomes Way More Powerful When You *Prove It!*
Show people that you understand where they are, what they want and, most importantly, who they are.

Use words and tell stories to pace their reality, and make it clear that you *get* them.

This is fantastically powerful as it shows them that *you live in their world.*
Remember everyone exists in their own reality – their own interpretation of

the world coloured by their own beliefs, prejudices, fears and desires. People are not in Rapport unless you are both speaking from the same *reality.*

When creating change, your ultimate goal will be to get them to join you in your reality.

BUT

Before you can bring them into your world,

you must first join them in theirs! In order to

do this, make it clear that you are right there

with them.

Of course, BEFORE you can do this, you have to actually BE right there. So *listen,*
engage, and put yourself in their shoes.

Use your imagination (you have one!) and see where it takes you.

*BTW, for more info on the idea of people's reality (or "Maps of the World") see my report called "**The Problem Shaker**" which I have included for you as a bonus appendix to this book.*

2. Fake It!

You know what it's like when you're in rapport.

You've been there thousands of times before, with friends, family and others that you get on with.

Inside your mind you already have the "Rapport Blueprint."

So, in order to create rapport deliberately, remember and *revivify* the feelings that you get when you are naturally in rapport with your friends.

Do this in a safe context first. At home, practice filling yourself with the feelings that you get when you're in rapport.

Mentally remember the times that you've had when you've felt easy and powerful connections with others.

Focus first on the memory, then identify the *feeling* and focus instead on that.

Practice bringing this feeling to life with ease, and keep exercising those mental muscles until you can make that feeling happen "on demand", whenever and wherever you want it to.

This gives you the keys to generating instant rapport at your beck and call!

How this works

The *feeling* of rapport isn't some weird magic ether that inexplicably affects those around you.

It's actually very simple.

Obviously the way you *feel* affects the way you *behave.*

When you're feeling grumpy, you act different to when you're feeling happy!

Your posture will naturally change, the tone of your voice will naturally change, your gestures and rate of speech will naturally change.

Even your *words* will naturally change depending on the emotional state that you're in.

Faking it at first makes everything just happen automatically, as your subconscious mind carries on these complex yet powerful processes without you even having to think about it!

3. "Always Be the Calmest Person in the Room"

My friend Marcus Oakey from

YourCharismaCoach.com taught me a

powerful lesson in Rapport and Persuasion:

"Always be the calmest person in the room."

The calmest person is the most in control, the person who feels the most at home, and the person who feels the most secure.

People don't like to connect with agitated people because those feelings poison the interaction, so as you focus on increasing the feelings of rapport, also make a conscious effort to become *calm.*

It becomes easier with practice– make it your intention to always be the calmest person in the room, and the dividends this will pay you will be *huge.*

Remember, calm doesn't mean dull! You can be animated, energetic and excited whilst still being calm and relaxed. Just don't be ruled by nervousness or stress, and don't let your feelings be buffeted around by those you're with.

The calmest person in the room is the most powerful person in the room, and the one that everyone else wants to be in rapport with!

Be the calmest person in the room, and others will try and create rapport with *you,*
putting the ball squarely (or roundly, as I've never met a square ball!) in your court.

4. Become a "People Person."
It's easy not to like people.

We have a lot of faults, and identifying them via a snap judgement when we meet someone new is human nature.

Oscar Wilde once said *"a cynic is someone who knows the value of everything but the price of nothing."*

It's so much easier to connect with people and influence them if you actually like them! For some of us this actually takes some training. Train yourself – it's worth it.

OK!

Ok, that's the four step rapport formula.
It's not so much four steps as it is four elements.

Make them all part of your word, and rapport will be easy, effortless and natural.

These four steps are some of the most powerful things I've learned on my journey towards mastering conversational hypnosis, and they will treat you very well indeed.

Voice Control: How to Sound Irresistibly Persuasive

PHEW! I hear some of you sigh.

We've now laid the foundations for successful persuasion, and it's time to build the sky scraper.

The foundations that we've laid so far are life changing.

Now it's time to build on what we have created, and look at the external techniques and behaviours to conversationally hypntize and persuade.

Ever seen a romantic comedy?

If you have, you'll no doubt have come across the phrase (said tearfully by a distraught heroine):

"It's not what you said, it's the way you said it!"

Funnily enough, she was right.
How you sound when you talk is at *least* as important as what you actually say. The way you project your voice carries a host of undertones and implications. Some people seem to naturally have pleasant voices, and others don't.

Fortunately with a little practice it's actually extremely easy to speak with a voice that projects authority and confidence, that is pleasant to listen to, and that commands attention.

Politicians realize with. When the famous former British Prime Minister, Margaret Thatcher, was leader of the opposition, she was often mocked for her shrill sounding voice.

There's a story about her campaign manager bumping into the voice coach of the legendary Shakespeare actor Laurence Olivier on a train, and begging him to train the future Prime Minister to speak more persuasively.

He agreed, and Thatcher went on to govern Britain for over a decade.

The Two Keys to a Persuasive Voice
1. Project from down low, not up high.

When most people talk, they project their voice from their mouth, their nose, their throat or their chest.

When they project from their throat or mouth, they sound high pitched and whiny. When they project from their nose, they sound nasal and unpleasant.

Project from your chest and you'll sound 'normal' – but we can do better than 'normal!'

Try this for an exercise that's been doing the rounds lately and is a fantastic way to understand how to project your voice.

The Voice Projection Exercise

When you're alone and somewhere you can

speak out loud without feeling,
embarrassed, do this:

Point to your nose, and speak exaggeratedly as if
you were projecting from your nose and say *"this
is my nose."*

Next point to your mouth, and speak exaggeratedly
as if you were projecting from your throat, and say
"this is my mouth."

Do the same for your throat, chest and belly.

Notice that when you project from your belly,
you take deeper breaths, you speak slower, and
your voice is more *calm*, powerful and measured.

That is how you should talk – practice projecting
from your belly and this alone will amplify and
supercharge the persuasiveness of how you talk!

2.   The Command Tones In basic

English communication, there are three

core inflections. The upward inflection

at the end of a sentence indicates a

question. An even or level inflection

indicates a statement – a normal

sentence. A downward inflection

indicates a command.

Try saying this sentence with the three different inflections, and notice the different implications it seems to carry:

"Today is a work day?"

"Today is a work day."

"Today is a work day!"

Notice the difference?

I recently started the mammoth task of trying to learn Chinese! It isn't easy, but it's fascinating.

Mandarin Chinese is a tonal language. Simple one syllable words can have literally dozens of meanings depending on where you place the inflection.

English is a lot easier.

Practice projecting your voice from the belly and using the command tonality when you want to create action.

The other tonalities are useful as well of course, but the command tonality is key, because it's the one that really indicates authority, and therefore motivates people and gets them to do stuff.

When changing the way you project your voice, a lot of you will be breaking the habits of a lifetime.

That's ok! The rewards will pay off in phenomenal droves as you notice people responding to you on deeper and more meaningful levels, and responding more readily to what you say.

Interpreting the Silent Story of Body Language

Scores of books have been written on how to

read and interpret body language. They teach

you that this gesture 'means' this and this

posture 'means' that.

Whilst this can sometimes be accurate, in the real world when you're in the middle of a dynamic, fast moving conversation, getting out your translation book and trying to codify every movement is not really practical.

Instead, understand where body language comes from, and why people make the significant gestures that they do, and you'll be able to 'read people like a book' without really having to think.

In order to understand this, transport yourself back to the dawn of human nature.

In an ancient tribal hunter / gatherer society where all instinctive habitual body language began to be shaped, the messages were very simple.

They all related to two things:

Territory and Safety.

When people are confident, they mean to portray their dominance by occupying more territory and proving their safety.

They'll sit in a wide open posture, occupying a large amount of the seat and exposing vulnerable areas, such as the neck, the belly and the crotch.

This proves that they feel safe and are unafraid of attack. It shows that they 'run the show' and are comfortable where they are.

They'll walk tall and at a slow, relaxed pace, as they're unafraid of being seen or spotted by enemies.

When they gesture it will be measured and relaxed, as they have no nervous or agitated energy.

These gestures of confidence portray leadership and authority.

When people are unconfident, however, they aim to protect themselves and occupy as little territory as possible.

They'll sit bent up and hunched over in a small corner of the seat. They'll cross their legs and fold their arms so as to protect vulnerable areas, maybe nervously scratching their neck so as to protect this region too.

They'll walk briskly, and stare at the ground so as to avoid making eye contact.

Their gestures will be erratic and nervous, and they'll

fidget or squirm with nervous energy.

That's the most basic story of body language, and we can see it all around as today.

We cover, of course, and often try and deliberately overcompensate for the gestures we try and display.

A teenager sprawled over an enormous park bench is a classic example of deliberate overcompensation for unconfident feelings.

Body language is not black and white. One unconfident signs mean nothing. Look for combinations of signals that build up a narrative and feed into the story this person is subconsciously and silently telling with their body.

Territory and space is not the only story told, but this theme of confidence, safety and dominance is an all consuming one.

Train your eyes to notice this constant non-verbal story, and you'll be amazed by how prevalent it is!

How to Speak Hypnotically: Language Patterns and Beyond

One of the most interesting things derived from NLP's study of the famous hypnotherapist Milton H Erickson is the *hypnotic language patterns.*

The patterns are ways to structure your language that enables you to communicate on multiple levels and therefore influence the subconscious mind, without conscious interference.

Like all 'hypnotic techniques', this is not some weird ninja 'woowoo' tool that has 'magic powers.' It's simply a codified break down of what naturally persuasive people do anyway.

How to use hypnotic language patterns without sound crazy...

The key to using hypnotic language is not just to know how to use them, but how to use them naturally so that they fit in with the normal rhythms of a conversation, and you don't sound like a whacko...

Here's an article for Keys To The Mind about a year prior to the publication of this book which explains it perfectly.

About 40 years ago, a linguist named John Grinder and a computer programmer named Richard Bandler sat down with a pen and paper, and set about picking apart the conversational patterns of a man named Milton Erickson.

Milton Erickson was a therapist and hypnotist based in Phoenix, Arizona, with a few unusual knacks.

Erickson noticed that when his clients came to see him, they often phrased their problems in strange ways. They'd speak in such a way that their totally irrational problems somehow seemed real, concrete and unchangeable.

Dr. Erickson thought that if these patterns kept people trapped inside problems, then they could probably be used to free people from problems as well.

He began talking to clients in that same language, feeding their patterns back to them. Patterns like...

***The Bind**, two ideas linked together: "the more you read about language patterns, the more you notice people using them naturally in everyday speech"...*

***The Double Bind**, the illusion of choice ... "people find they either find language patterns easy to use or simple to implement in their daily communication"...*

***Presuppositions**... "when (presupposition of - me, it's not if, it's when) you realize (presupposition of awareness, it's not whether it's happening, it's whether you've noticed) how easy it is to use these language patterns,* *you'll notice that you've already made massive changes in the way you communicate"...*

Embedded Commands*... When you read this post you'll discover more ways to use these patterns in your interactions...*

Cause – Effect patterns,*... Reading this post means you're learning about hypnotic language patterns, and because you're learning these patterns, it means you can use them naturally in your everyday interactions.*

And a lot more besides! Grinder and Bandler broke down these patterns, and called the model they created "The Milton Model."

The patterns aren't logical, but they play into the way the mind thinks, and create a compelling motivation for actions and beliefs.

The Milton Model is today used by therapists, businessmen, marketers and more to connect with people, change their beliefs and attitudes, and motivate them to take action, and create change.

How To Use Hypno-c Language Patterns without Sounding Crazy...

There are those who say language patterns are absurd, that they could never possibly be used in a real life conversation, and are at best a crutch for the anxious or nervous hypnotist.

They assume that in order to use language patterns in normal conversations, you have to drastically change the way you speak.
Here's the secret: you don't!

The fact is, language patterns are used by us in our everyday lives, all the -me! The trouble is, they're normally used for negative things.

Every -me someone says " I've realized I'll either fail now, or give
up" (presupposition of awareness followed by a double bind), or " the more I talk to him, the more annoyed I get" (bind), they are using language patterns!

Open your ears, and you'll find people use patterns of the Milton Model all the time! They are a natural function of English language communication!

So, rather than allowing us to trap ourselves into our problems with these patterns, why not use them to help free our minds, get what we want from life, and help others do the same?

Keep an ear out for language patterns in your everyday interactions, and ask yourself how you can use these patterns for the results you want.

Ok, so hopefully now you have a good idea of what language patterns are, how they work, and how to use them without being locked up.

There are lots of online materials dealing with language patterns, but if you seriously want to step up your game, I suggest you go grab the old NLP book "Patterns of the Hypnotic Techniques of Milton H Erickson M.D Volume 1."

It's not an easy read, but if you can get your head around that and integrate the techniques into what you do, you'll safely be able to say that you've mastered hypnotic language patterns!

The "Shiny Objects" Trap

At the end of this book in the second bonus appendix I give you 20 hypnotic phrases that all incorporate these hypnotic language patterns and more.

At this stage, however, I'm not going to spend more time on language patterns in this book, and here's why:

I believe they get a disproportionate amount of attention in this field due to what I call the "shiny objects" trap.

Language patterns *seem* very cool! A tricky little phrase or technique designed to wrap someone's mind up in a hypnotic loop and influence them on the subconscious level.

And yes, learning and mastering hypnotic language patterns is a very useful skill... HOWEVER everything else you learn in this book will increase your persuasive powers 100X more than any fancy patterns.

If you want to focus more on language patterns, please be my guest! Do a Google search for this phrase:

Hypnotic Language Patterns

And a bunch of links will appear teaching you hypnotic language patterns.

In this book, however, we can do better.

So if you'll permit me to move on, let's focus on a technique which is far more powerful than hypnotic language patterns, and is the key to irresistible influence and effortless conversational influence:

Hypnotic Stories That Change Minds and Shape Emotions

The way to a man (or woman's) heart is through *story.*
Stories are all around us, and form the bedrock of how we shape our beliefs, and even our identities.
Political candidates run for election based on the *narrative* they tell about their lives and how it ties in with the *narrative* of the country they are hoping to run.

President Obama once even said that one of the biggest jobs an American President has is to tell the American people an overarching story that relates the events of the world and the country, to the lives of the regular people.

You are living your own personal narrative.

What you think about yourself – your strengths, weaknesses and so on – all have their root in a *story* that you tell yourself.

These stories aren't factual, and they aren't *real*. Rather, they are remembered and interpreted by you, and spun and framed so that they support and feed the beliefs you have shaped for yourself.

Successful people tell themselves a story about how they learn, overcome failure, grow and succeed.

Unsuccessful people tell themselves a story about how the world is against them, and they lack the skills or opportunities others have.

In order to influence somebody and really connect with them, you have to understand *story.*

Since the dawn of civilisation *story* has shaped and defined the human species. Written or spoken, stories define a culture and a family, a friendship or marriage, work relationship and even a building or artwork or song.

If you don't understand story, you don't understand life!

So how do you use the power of story to influence others and change minds, and tap into this incredible force that flows through all of us?

One of the most powerful and persuasive ways is to use stories that mirror the situation that someone else is in, without directly referencing it.

This is the key behind what people call *therapeutic metaphor.*

An Example of Problem Solving Metaphor

Today I took a break from writing this book to grab a coffee (or green tea in my case actually since it's late!) with an old friend from where I grew up.

He was a bit down on his luck and was struggling to motivate himself to get out of a rut.

Rather than giving him a motivational speech and preaching life lessons (never a good look!) I gently changed the subject and told a story about my trip to China earlier on this year.

I told about being totally lost and confused in strange bustling cities, and having to completely figure things out as I went, despite being totally out of my depth.

The point I was making was that when you get the courage to drop yourself in a strange and challenging situation, you will amaze yourself with your own resourcefulness, and always find a way to pull through.

The story I told mirrored his situation – fear to leave his comfort zone and challenge himself – but was interesting and removed enough for me to get in all the lessons without directly having to say or do anything.

Discovering Your Own Personal Bank of Stories

Even if you think you live an 'ordinary' life, you still have a wealth of stories to use to motivate, inspire, and persuade others.

The key is to search for common themes that will be useful for you as a persuader.

Saying something through story is much more persuasive than just saying something directly. Plus, telling stories is intrinsically good!

When you get good at telling stories which enthrall and entertain, people will not be able to help but hang off your every word!

So first of all, become an observer of stories, both things that happen to you, and things that you read and see on TV.

Develop a journalist's eye for a tale and ear for a quirk.

Discover interesting characters in your life, and read weird and wonderful books.

Think just about the last week of your life and ask yourself, what events / stories / ideas / people did you meet / watch / read or hear about that demonstrate the following.

- Overcoming a problem

- Finding resources you didn't know you had

- Learning something new

- Gaining new energy

- Changing your world view

- Finding pleasure in life

Even everyday events can be powerful stories. I recently sent my email newsletter a story about my cat and how she behaves whenever I get back from an overseas trip.

Her behaviour – shunning me at first as 'punishment' for leaving then eventually forgiving me – was a perfect metaphor for the message I was trying to impart.
Stories are everywhere. Become a collector of stories and a compulsive storyteller. The only way to get good and develop your own style is to practice. Make a real effort to tell a story in all significant interactions you have, and see what effect they have.

You'll be stunned by just how much people *long* for a good story, and how even the most trivial and commonplace of everyday occurrences can become a powerful and persuasive story if you let it.

Telling a powerful story

When you tell a story, it's essential that you lose yourself in it. Transport yourself there, and you'll take your listeners with you!

Talk in multiple senses; use sight, sound, feelings and even tastes and smells (if appropriate) to totally make the scene you're creating come alive.

When you first start out as a story teller, ***get carried away!***

If you start out going over the top and getting carried away by the energetic exuberance of your own storytelling, that's great!

From that starting point you can gradually reign yourself in as you gain more experience, and develop that subtlety, reserve and finesse that really marks a master storyteller.

But, you have to start off up in the air!

Throw your inhibitions to the wind and immerse yourself in the world you are creating with your words.

As you do so, you'll be observing what works and gradually shaping your style to remove what you don't need, while refining what you're good at.

Before you know it, you'll be telling stories that will have people hanging off your every word!

Belief Shifting Questions That Rapidly Alter Ideas and Perspectives

Creating change and *persuading* others often boils down to shifting *beliefs.* Beliefs are often the 'underlying reason' behind a particular behaviour or resistance.

If you want someone to do something, they must believe certain things;

- That they are capable of it

- That they will benefit from it

- That their peers will approve of it

- That it isn't dangerous

These are not set in stone of course, but it's a good barometer of the basic underlying beliefs that modulate our actions.

Any subtle negative belief that fits into one of the four above categories could kill your chances of successful persuasion.

- If someone believed that they aren't capable of becoming a persuasive person, they wouldn't have invested in this book!

- If someone believed that this book was written by a quack with a crystal meth addiction, and that the secrets won't benefit them, they wouldn't have bought this book!

- If someone believed that people would judge them for wanting to increase their effectiveness as a communicator, they would have thought twice before buying this book!
- If someone thought these techniques and principles of effective persuasion were *illegal* and may get them arrested (ie put them in danger) then they wouldn't have bought this book!

Questions are a subtle and indirect way to change negative beliefs and eliminate them without directly attacking them.

Unfortunately, our instinctive reaction when someone confronts us with a belief we want to remove is to challenge the belief directly.

Unfortunately, this belief may be crucial to someone's identity and self image – even if it's a negative one.

Even if the belief is irrational, they will do all they can to justify and rationalize this belief that you have challenged, committing themselves to it and therefore making it much stronger.

The best way to change a belief is to make them think that changing the belief was
their idea.

That's where the art of questions come in.

With questions you can gradually loosen someone's grip on a negative belief, and move to replace it with a more positive, empowering belief set instead.

Five Powerful Question Types That Bust Unwanted Beliefs

Some of these questions come from NLPs 'meta model.'

The meta model is often overlooked in persuasion texts, but it's at least as powerful and useful as the famous language pattern based Milton Model.

The meta model allows you to identify the real thought patterns that a belief is wrapped up in, and gently ease that belief to the surface.

The meta model was enhanced by the 'sleight of mouth patterns' a belief change system that also forms part of the NLP sphere.

All of these questions eventually aim to sever the belief from the person, and break their attachment to it.

Remember, *it's not what you say, it's HOW you say it.*
Ask these questions like a challenging lawyer in the court room kind of way, and you'll just put people's backs up.

Ask them instead from a place of *genuine curiosity.* Be completely open, and allow them to give a clear and honest response without feeling judged or accused.

You're not out to prove that their beliefs are wrong. Instead you're kindly allowing them to realize *for themselves* that these beliefs are not only unhelpful, but that they also don't have to be stuck with them for life.

Important: One question alone will seldom work instant magic. Gradually and gently guide the questions by layering these questions and similar ones until the belief is shaken.

This should eventually lead to an epiphany moment when they begin to reorient their perspective.

When the old belief is lost, begin using *story* to inspire and create a new belief that is the opposite solution to the old one.

Walk Through

Someone has a negative belief.

You carefully and gradually use the questions below to loosen the belief to the point where they no longer have that same attachment to it.

When the belief is loose, subtly use stories (see the previous segment) that mirror the situation to inspire the *new* belief – confidence instead of unconfidence, good instead of bad.

Allow them to get acquainted with the new belief, as this has to firmly take the place of the old.

In a real interaction you'll be running with your instincts. This is why it's crucial that you're in rapport the whole time.

If you break rapport to try and think of 'what was that hypnotic question again?' you risk losing the potential to create change, so tread carefully.

Remember, the change was *their* idea, so don't go claiming credit! **The Questions:**

1. The Counter Example Question

Get them to gradually begin to mentally formulate counter examples of the belief that they have.

You could ask:

- *"What are the situations in which (belief) is not true?*

- *"When was the last time that you acted (contrary to belief)?"*

- *"What's the most (opposite of belief) thing that you've done recently"*

- *"Who is more (belief) / less (opposite of belief) than you?"*

You're guiding them to build up a mental catalogue of situations in which this belief was false, gradually making it less real.

2. The Source Question

Ask people where they got that negative belief from. The goal of this is to show them that *they* are not the source of the negative belief, that it's not really something that they chose to create for themselves.

"Who first told you (belief)"

"How long have you believed that...?"

3. The Usefulness Challenge

The usefulness challenge accomplishes two things.

First, it begins to dissociate the belief from reality by having the person view it as a
belief, not as a fact.

Second it begins to get them to want to emotionally distance themselves from this belief.

The goal is to get them to realize that it's not the FACT of the negative belief that has hindered them; it's the fact THAT THEY BELIEVE IT.

I.e. it's not the fact that someone is shy that hinders them, it's the fact that they
believe they are.

"Is it useful to believe that?" "Does believing this help you?"
"Has this belief ever gotten in your way?"

4. The Elimination Question

Building on the previous question, this question has them mentally create a world in which this belief does not exist.

This allows them to begin the process of replacing the

negative belief with a positive one, and helps them start building a reality that is not dependent upon the negativebelief.

- *"How different would you feel if you believed the opposite?"*

- *"What would you do in (situation) if you believed (opposite)?"*

- *"Imagine what would happen in your life if you believed (opposite)?*

5. The Overcoming Question

In this question you have them give you their supposed criteria for overcoming this belief.

You can work with this criteria if it's useful to you, or move beyond it.

This question causes them to give you a clear road map for overcoming the negative belief, so can be extremely useful.

Like the previous two questions, it emphasizes the dissociation between fact and belief, and begins getting their mind whirring towards the elimination of this belief.

- *"What would it take for you to suddenly stop believing this?"*

- *"If you were to suddenly stop believing this, what would make that happen?"*

- *"How easy would it be for you to suddenly*

believe (opposite)?"

That's It!

As you use these questions, you'll understand the principles behind them and the subtle mechanics at play on a deeper level.

Soon, you'll find yourself naturally using them in conversations AND with yourself to bust negative beliefs without you even having to think about it.

Remember no technique is an island.

Combine questions with stories and hypnotic language patterns whilst speaking persuasively and coming from a solid inner game foundation, and there'll be absolutely no stopping you.

Be sure to read the bonus appendix on "The Problem Shaker", which I have included in this book, as it will demonstrate many of the principles at play here for you in a real world setting.

Conclusion: Cancelling the Contradictions

We're coming to the end of this book!

Relax though, in the bonus section you'll find
a bunch of potent and practical material to
help you bring out your skills into the real
world.

Already, you're miles further ahead than

when you began this short read. You know

how to speak with authority and

confidence.

You know how to read and interpret the silent story
of body language.

You know how to get out of your own way
and think and feel like a master persuader.

You know the secret to hypnotic language patterns.
You know how to tell powerful stories which enthrall
as they transform.

You know how to ask questions that destroy
negative beliefs, and flip problems on their head.

You know what Queen Victora, Steven R Covey
and Bernard Baruch had to say about how to
get your own way.

You know how to rapidly gain rapport with almost
anyone.

And, you know that this book has

contradicted itself at least once so far!

That's ok.

Remember all we are doing here is constructing *models.*

We're interpreting people and the world in a useful and empowering way.

These skills are effective, useful and most importantly, they work!

But they are not the 'be all and end all' of life and communication as a human being.

It's up to you – in your studies and, most importantly, in your experiences – to square the circles, fill in the gaps and reconcile the contradictions.

I wish you the best of luck, and sincerely hope that you've had as much fun reading this book as I did writing it.
So that's all,
Cheers

Bonus Appendix One: The Problem Shaker

If you've ever been talking to somebody who is down about some sort of problem or worry – maybe it's to do with work, or a relationship – and you have wanted tosnap them out of it and make them feel great, let me present you with perfect tool for the job.

Obviously, if you're a hypnotist or hypnotherapist, this technique will be a fantastic addition to your repertoire, and you can adapt it for almost any situation.

I call it "The Problem Shaker."

How "The Problem Shaker" Works...

If you've been on my newsletter for a while, you will have learned that your core inner game is the most important element of ANY hypnosis or influence work you do.

Of course, just because you're focusing on your core inner game, it doesn't mean that you can't use cool ninja strategies to conversationally hypnotize others.

BUT, rather than presenting a scripted 'technique' that may sound cool but that 9/10 of you would never try (and the other 1/10 would probably
fail) I want to install in you an attitude and mindset

that will do the work for you.

The Power of Intention

Sorry about the negative example – but this is the quickest way I can help you really get the power of what we're talking about here.

Have you ever been angry – furious, about someone or something, so angry that you could not control your words, and said something hurtful or mean?

That's OK! You're human, these things happen, and that's in the past.

I bring it up because it shows you how much impact your emotional state and intention can have on the way you communicate.

Now, imagine if you could have the OPPOSITE of that – a powerful positive intention so strong that you can't help but say the PERFECT thing, which helps other people (and yourself) to just feel great!

That is the problem shaker.

Lead From The Heart, and The Mind Will Follow

Relax – we're not getting into the realms of 'woo woo' weirdness here, but I do need you to understand that the bulk of your communication occurs at a subconscious level.

Your tonality, body language, gestures, breathing rate, and to a large extent even your word choice is subconscious.

So, it stands to reason that if you want to effectively influence somebody, you should work on your whole self, not just on the shallow conscious level.

This is what the problem shaker is all about.

While a general positive intention will serve you tremendously well, for the problem shaker I'd like to get very specific.

And it starts with a very precise emotional place...

The Monster In The Cupboard...

Imagine that you knew a reasonably bright kid of about 6 or 7, who was perfectly normal and happy, yet he was afraid of a monster in his bedroom cupboard.

Would you try and logically convince him that there was no monster there? Would you angrily tell him to grow up and get over it?
Would you freak out, and run out of the room, lest the monster eat you too?

These options may sound farcical – but emotional persuasion, anger or, even worse
– AGREEING with the problem – are the ways most people in most conversations try and help their friends out!

As this example should clearly show you, this does not help! So, what would you do?

You'd be calm, confident and friendly.

You joke around with the kid, and make him laugh at just how silly he was.

Maybe you'd get him to imagine a large pink monster with a Christmas hat on, and join him in his reality WITHOUT buying into his fear or negative emotions.

You'd be relaxed, playful and reassuring, and at the end of the chat the child would smile, relax, and be able to sleep without worry or fear.

Don't Buy Into Problem Frames

The key lesson from this is to NEVER buy into problem frames.

If someone comes to you and says "I just broke up with my boyfriend and now my life sucks" would you say "Aw, poor you. That's so terrible! I'm so sad for you?"

Sadly, without reading this article many people would!

But that's exactly the same as telling the 7 year old kid "Oh my god! A Monster! You're on your own kid, I'm getting out of here! "

When people are bogged down by a problem they are NOT seeing the world through a very productive frame of mind.

Joining them in their world view

is the worst thing you could do.

Instead, maintain YOUR frame.

YOUR frame should be the 'everything's

fine and life is awesome' frame. Project

this in every aspect of your

communication.

This shift alone will make you a much better problem solver than 90% of the rest of the world.

Join Them In Their Reality FIRST

Ouch! Have I just contradicted myself big time?

First I tell you "do NOT buy into their frame",
then I say join them in their reality first!

Well, actually the two work together.
Imagine that you are rescuing somebody from a
burning building.

Would you wander in as soon as you hear their
shouts, sit down on the flaming couch and burn
with them?

No!

But, you wouldn't stand outside and yell 'it's not
burning out here, don't be such a baby!' either,
would you?

The best thing to do would be to suit up in a
protective uniform, grab a fire hose, charge in,
grab them, and then get them out of there
quickly.

This is how you should treat helping someone out of
personal problems too.

Show Understanding Without Getting Burnt

People like to know that their problems are understood.

There's also a reason why NLP style pacing and leading works extremely well in many situations.

You can be bouncing off the walls with happiness, but if your mate is really down, your emotional level will be so far outside their reality that your message will not stand a chance of reaching them.

Before you pick them up, you must first bend down.

Realize that TO THEM their problems are real, but always REMEMBER that they are real ONLY TO THEM, and assert your reality, that actually, the world is just fine, thank you very much.

The Three Step Problem Shaker Formula

So, let's try and slap some logical

structure around these principles... 1:

Recognize that their problem is NOT

real. BUT it is real for them.

2: Join them in their reality just long enough to pull them out.

3: Refuse to buy into their negative emotions – maintain your positive frame, and keep them locked onto it too.

The Last Metaphor

I'm battling with the challenge of making the problem shaker principle clear to you without suffocating your creativity by giving you too many concrete   examples.

So, here's yet another metaphor.

Imagine you're on a nice warm dry boat, but

someone falls out into the water. Your friend

can't swim, and she's clearly going to drown.

How do you help her?

You could tell her that she must be crazy for thinking she's drowning, because the boat is just fine, thank you very much.

Sure, you aren't buying into her frame, but you aren't helping much either, are you?

You could jump in next to her, but seeing as you can't swim either (in this particular metaphor) you'd start drowning too.

This is buying into her frame too much.

You could shout at her to start swimming and stop being lazy.

This is advice giving – it almost never really helps.

Or, you could lean over, bend down, grasp her hand, and pull her out, then give her a warm towel, and a dry change of clothes.

This is joining her in her world (bending down and extending your hand) but maintaining your frame (staying on the boat and keeping dry), and pulling her into it (lifting her onto the boat).

This is how the problem shaker works.

Time To Get Started!

Right now, you might be feeling a little confused. That's ok – it's natural.

Usually when you learn things you are taught that confusion is bad – that's how the schooling system normally works.

You get confused, you make a mistake and you get punished.

Fortunately, learning how to be a master hypnotist and a better person is NOT like that.

We recognize that confusion is the gateway to new understandings.

Take from this article an attitude and mindset, and use it to BECOME a "Problem Shaker."

Bonus Appendix 2: Twenty "Magic Phrases" That Instantly Change Minds

Ok, I lied. These phrases aren't *magic,* but they are powerful. They subtly tie together many threads from this book into simple sentences.

In particular, they incorporate elements of persuasive questions and hypnotic language patterns.

See if you can spot what they're made of!

Remember I could break them down for you, but since this is an appendix I'll let you do the hard yards and internalize the ideas for yourself.

Remember: Don't get sucked into the "Shiny Object" trap! Yes these sentences are useful, but they are not magic spells to be waved on their own.

To use these in conversations, follow your own common sense and make sure you have every other element of this book down!

Obviously, adapt these phrases for your own purposes, and think about the layers and implications each one employs.

The 20 (not so) "Magic Phrases."

1. *The more you read this book, the more persuasive you become.*

2. *Reading this book causes you to become*

persuasive, which means this book is making you into a master persuader.

3. *Stop and consider all the times that you've said "Aha!" and had a powerful realization when reading this book.*

4. *If you knew about the lessons in this book when you were just a kid, just how popular would you have been at school?*

5. *When you re-read this book in a year's time, you'll look back on this moment as being the start of a wonderful transformation.*

6. *Whenever in the future you find yourself with a persuasive goal in mind, you'll be overcome with a sense of calm and confidence, as you do know exactly what to do, don't you?*

7. *Before you begin naturally integrating these persuasive patterns into your everyday speech, consider just how far you have come already without even realizing it!*

8. *Don't allow yourself to enjoy the full reach of your new persuasive powers until you relax, and allow yourself to persuade others without even having to try.*

9. *How does it make you feel to know that the more persuasive you become, the more the people around you find the resources to overcome their problems and live their lives to the fullest?*

10. Just stop right now and pretend and imagine that you were the most charismatic, confident and persuasive person on the planet. Now pretend that you had stopped pretending.

11. You don't have to believe that you're the most persuasive person on the planet because you don't have to believe that you have two hands, two feet and two ears – people will know this about you instantly as soon as they see you.

12. Are you paying close attention, or is your subconscious mind simplyabsorbing everything that you're reading without you even having to try?

13. I'm not sure whether you'll rapidly grow into a master persuader, or whether you'll simply realize that you had the resources you needed all along, you just needed to bring them to the surface.

14. Obviously you know that you've already learned far more about persuading others than you've even begun to realize.

15. Before you notice just how far you've already come as a persuader, imagine just how much further you're still going to go!

16. You'll often discover yourself using persuasive techniques without even trying. When you find this, realize it's a sign that you're on the right track!

17. Every time you use a persuasive technique,

you have succeeded in practicing your skills and are well on your way to success. If the technique works, that's just the icing on the cake.

18.*Have you ever wondered if people have already started to notice your new persuasive powers, even if you weren't aware of them yourself?*

19.*The easiest part about improving the way you communicate is that you get to improve the way you listen, therefore the people around you become better communicators.*

20. *I am the best hypnotist , now.*

www.ingramcontent.com/pod-product-compliance
Lightning Source LLC
Chambersburg PA
CBHW051359280526
45784CB00007B/3027